We hope you enjoy coloring this book.

Download some extra **free coloring patterns** and get news of upcoming books at

www.scribblepresscoloring.com/free-download

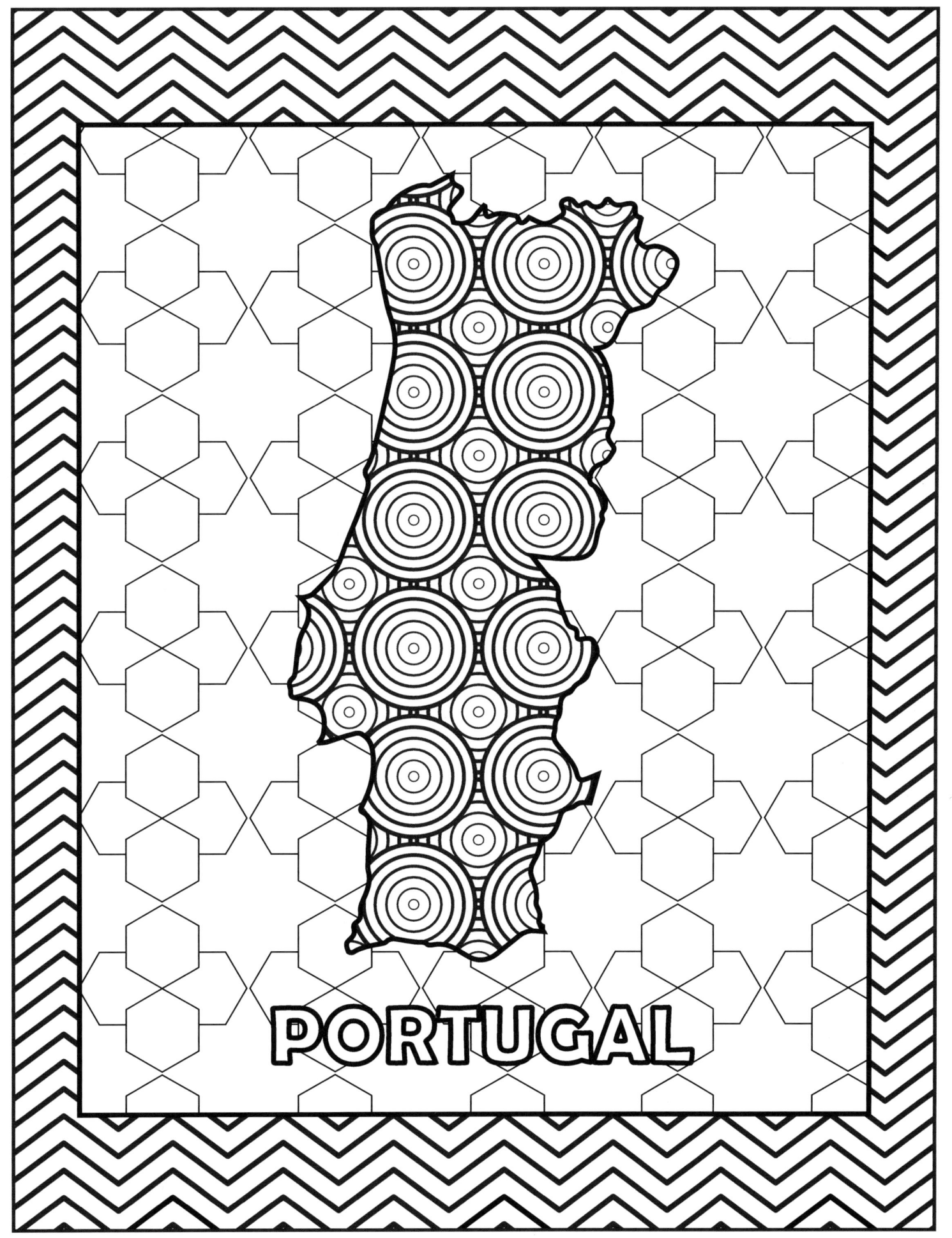

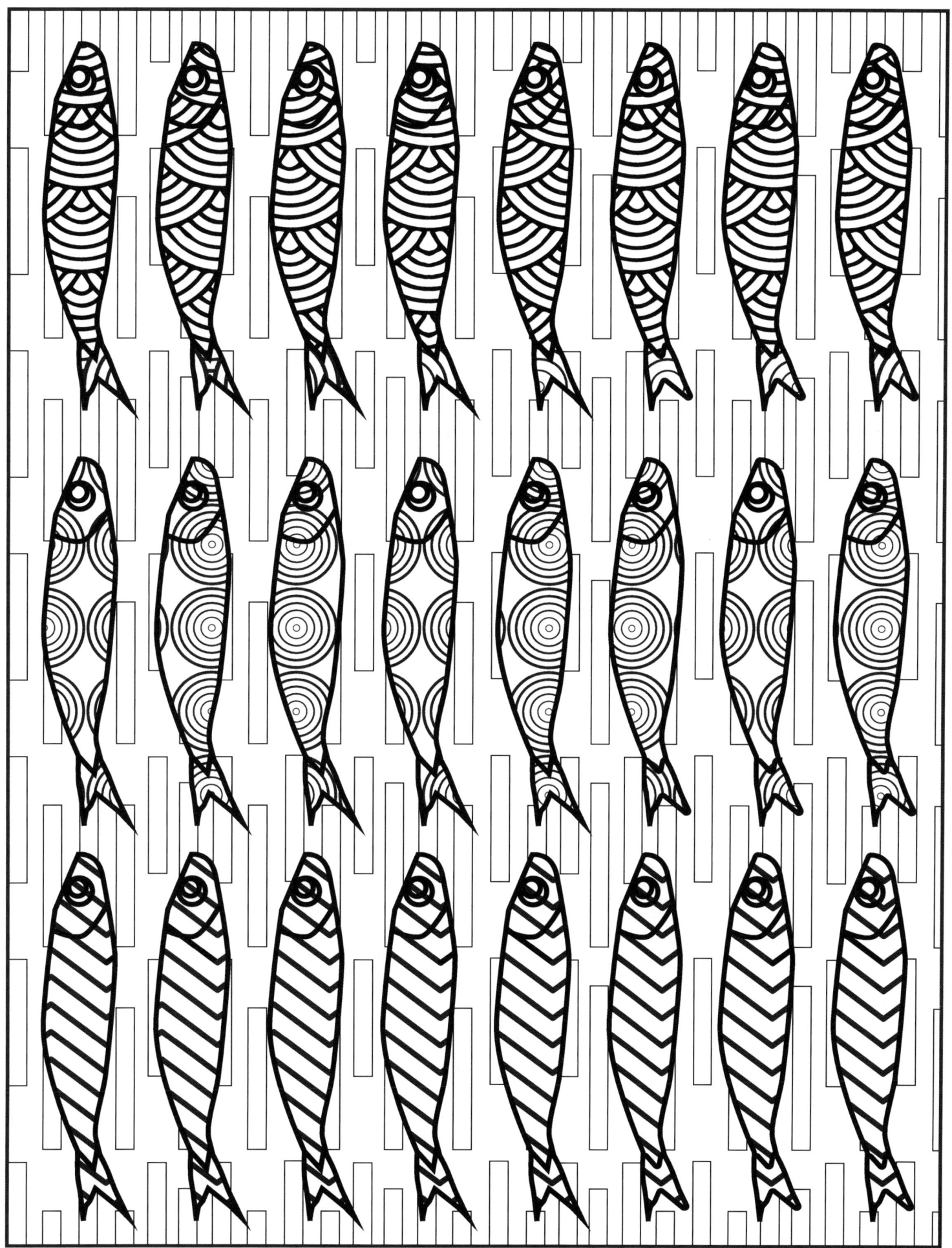

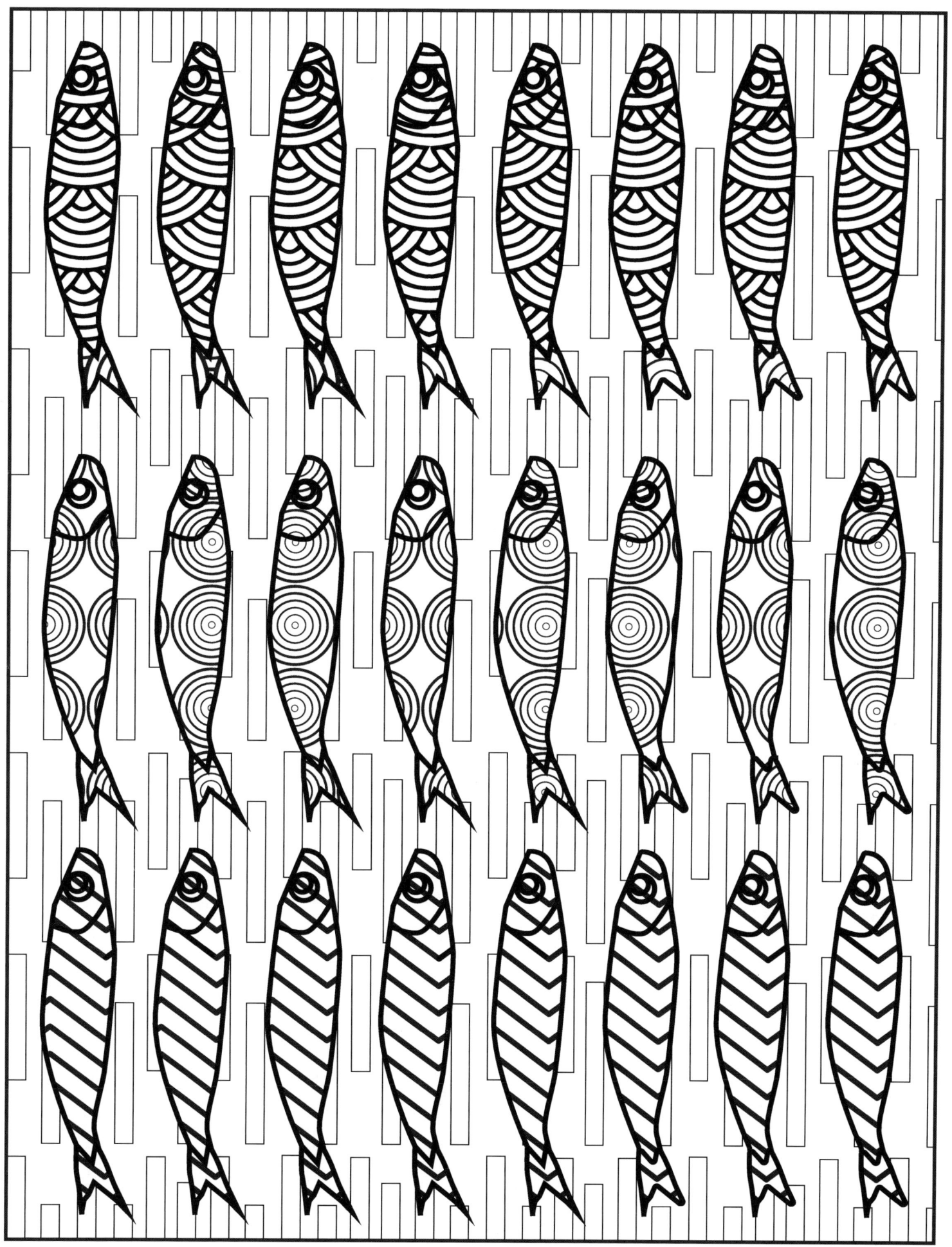

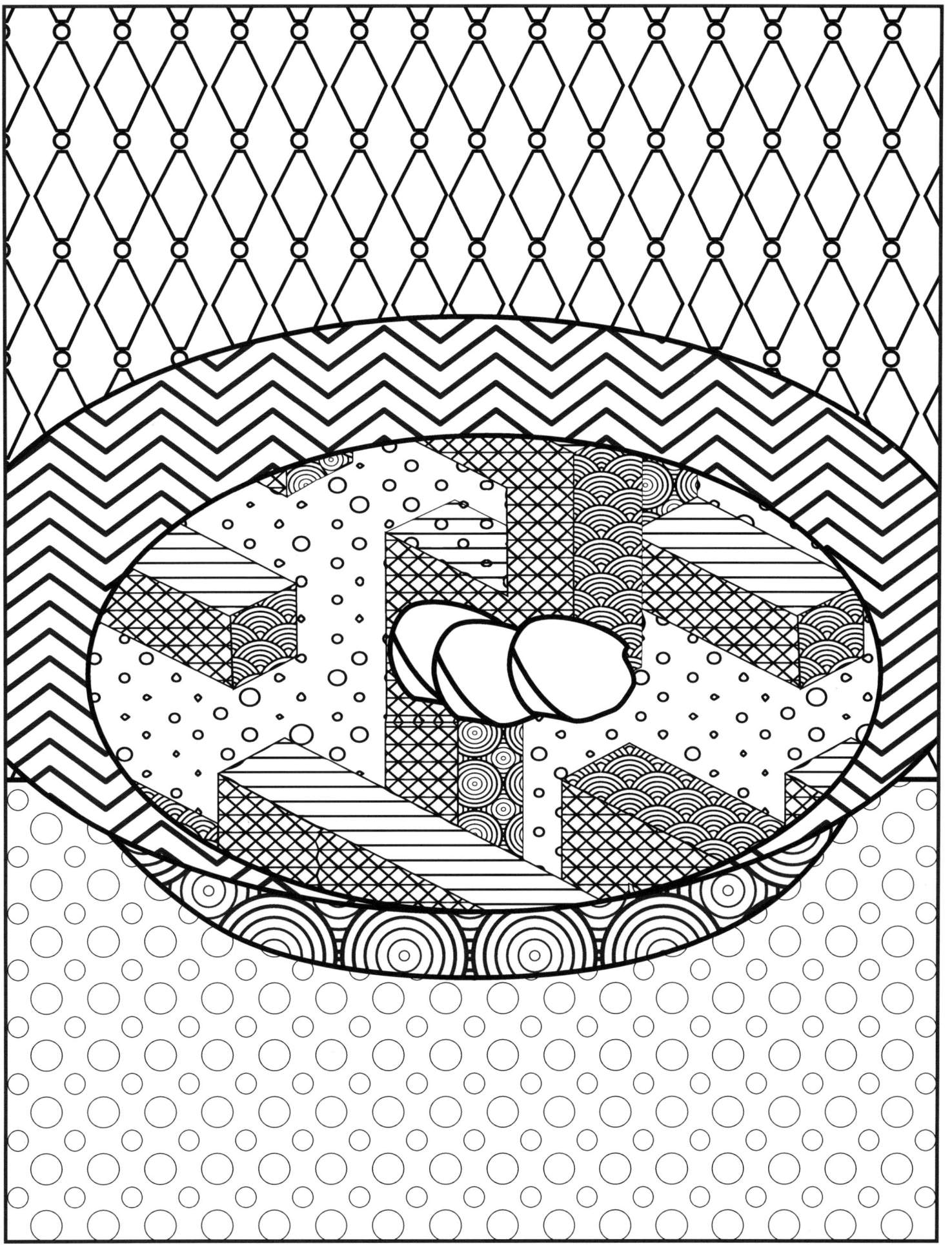

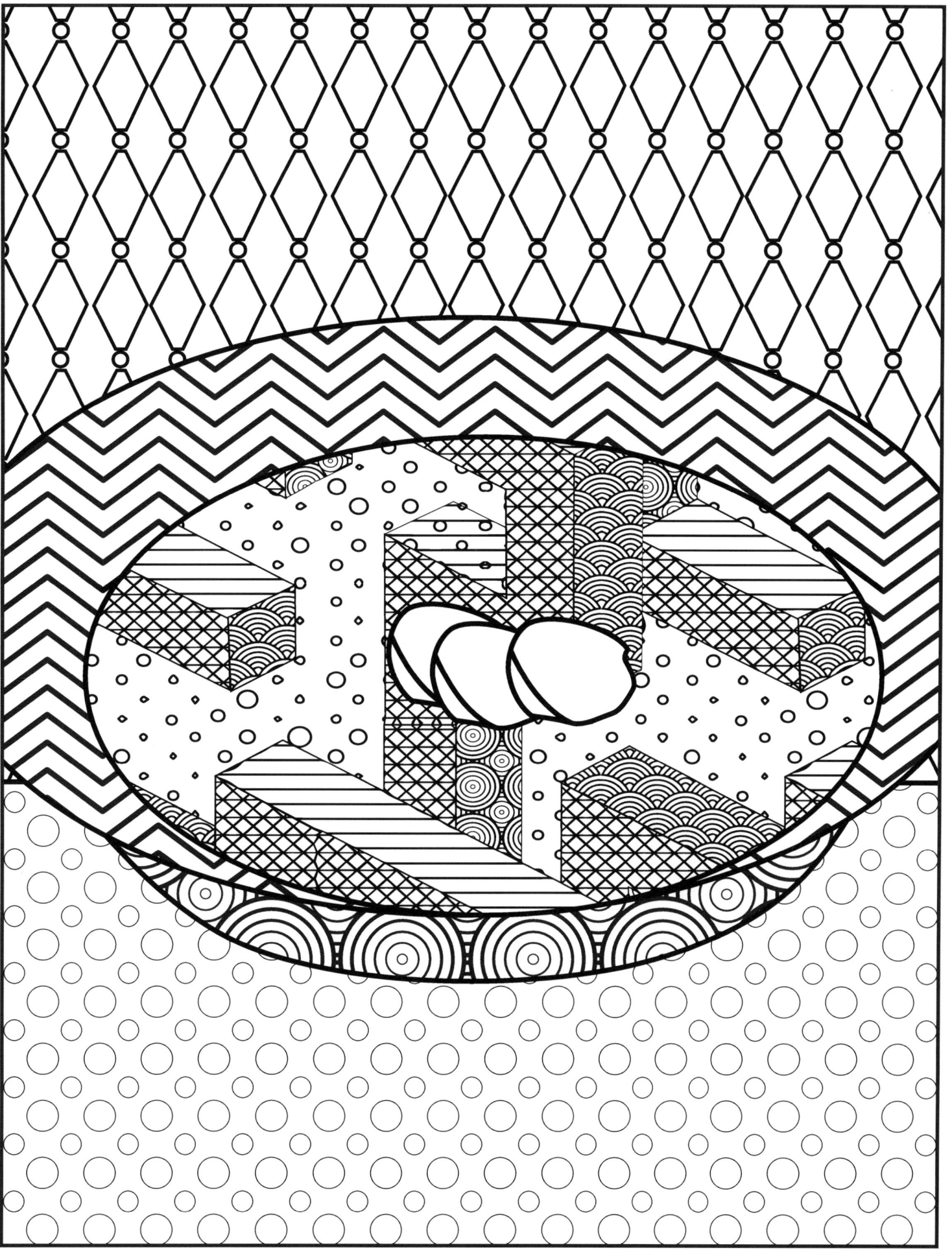

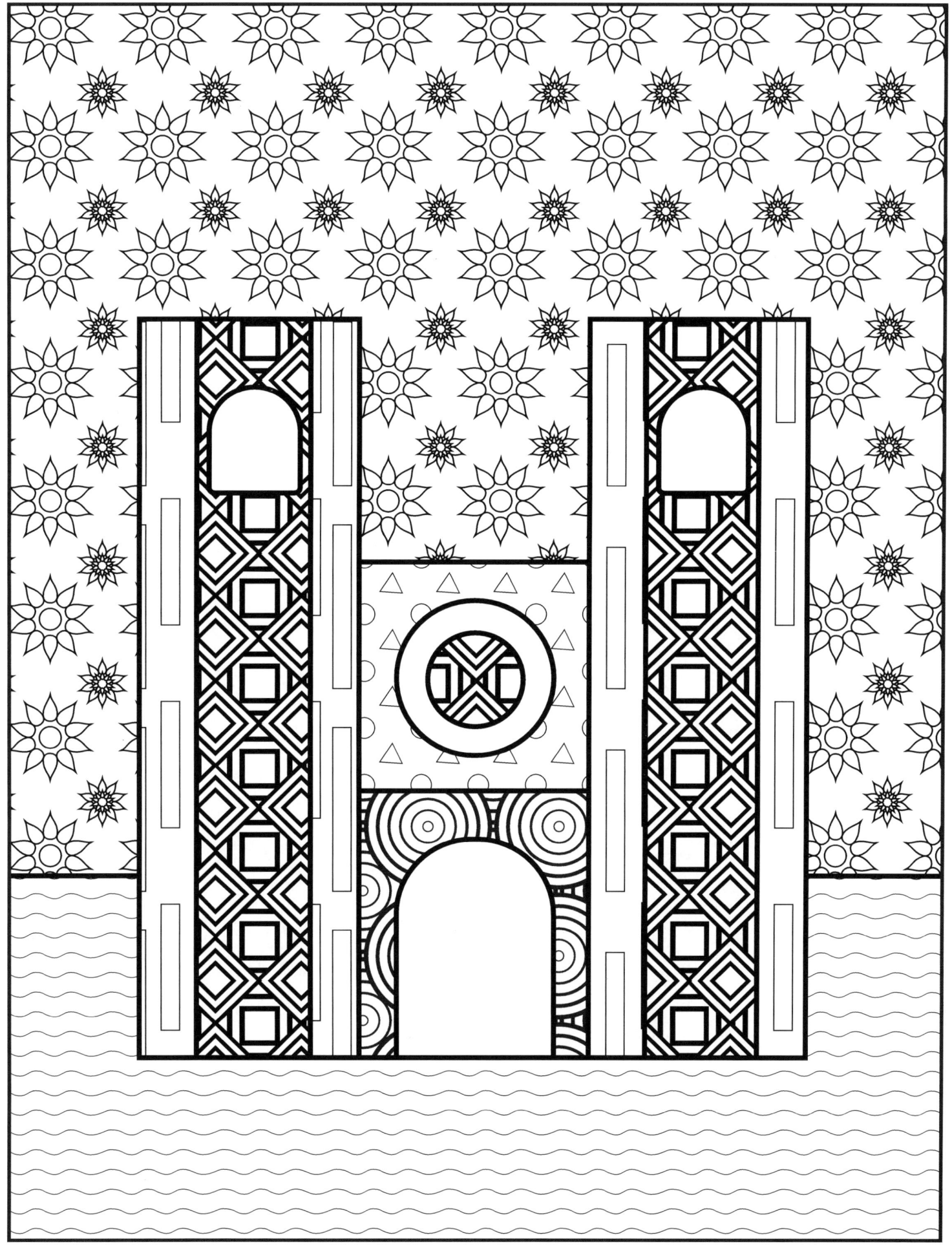

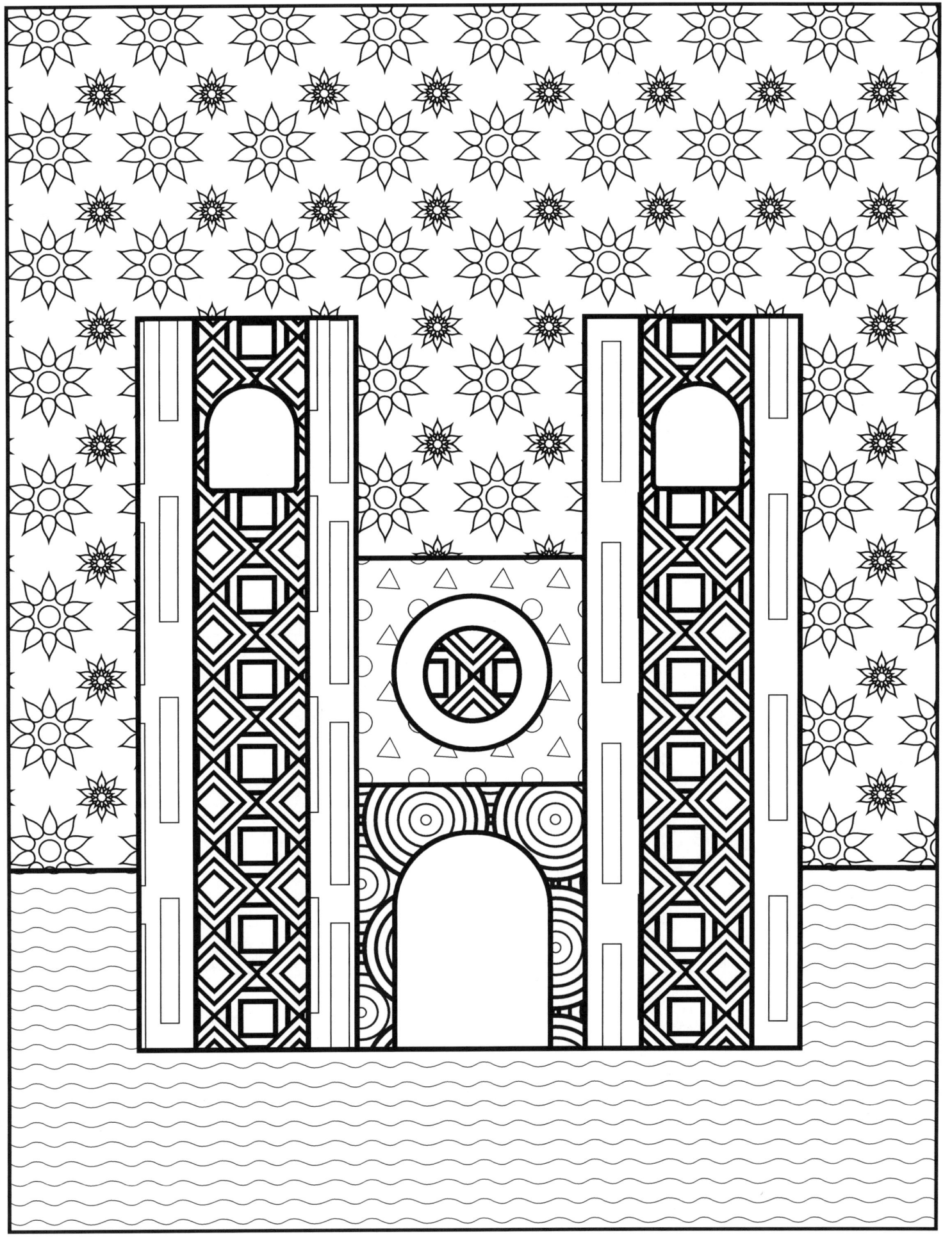

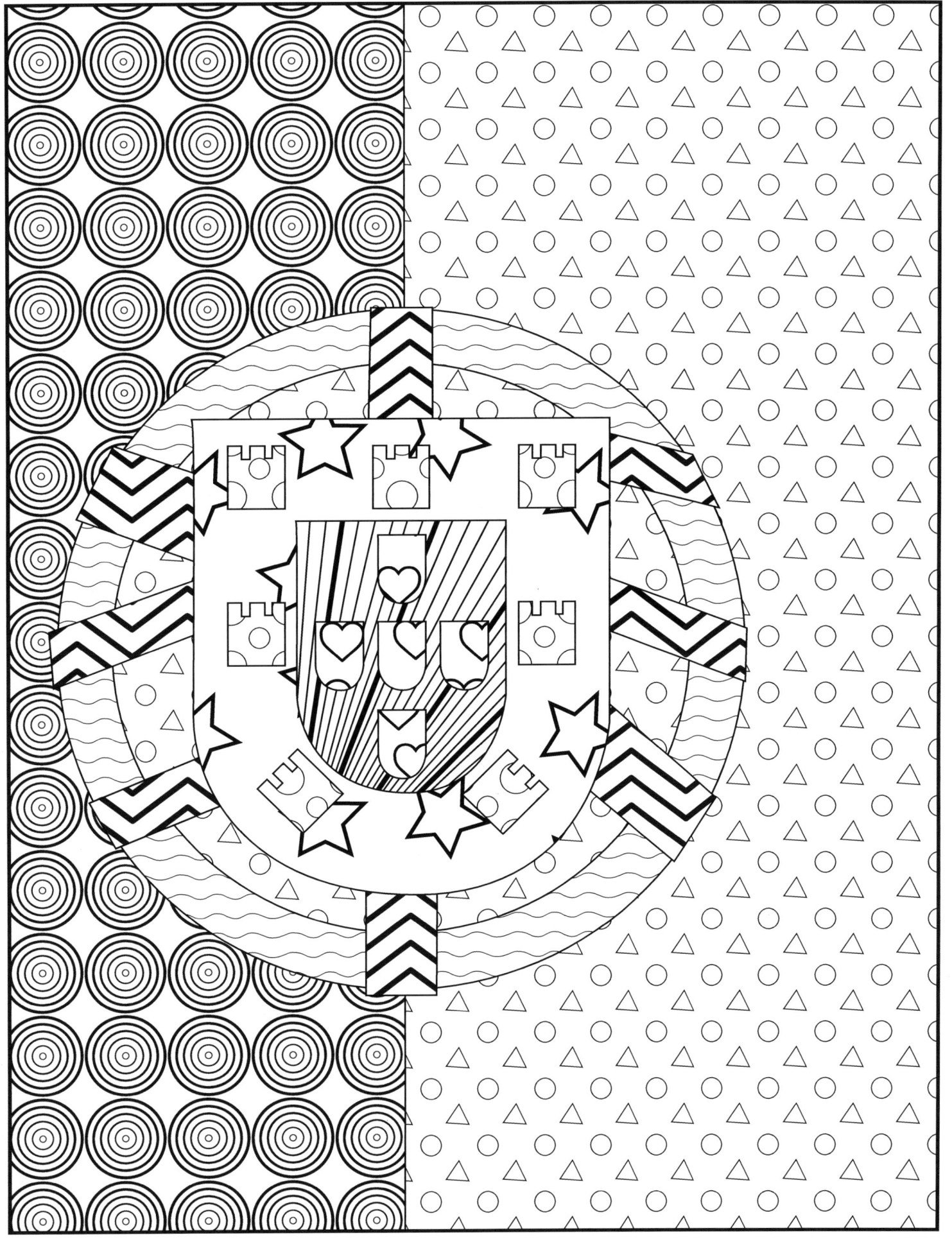

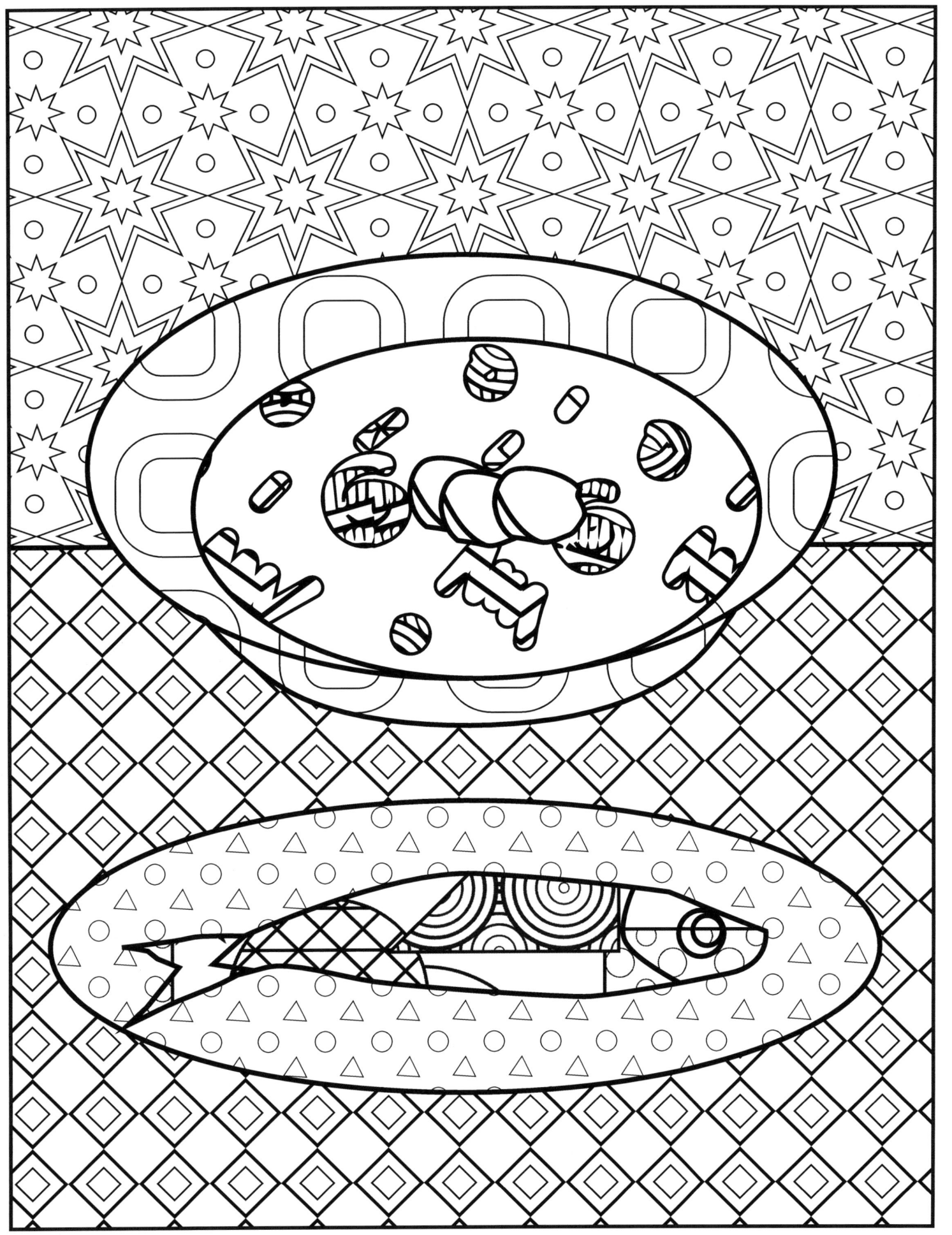

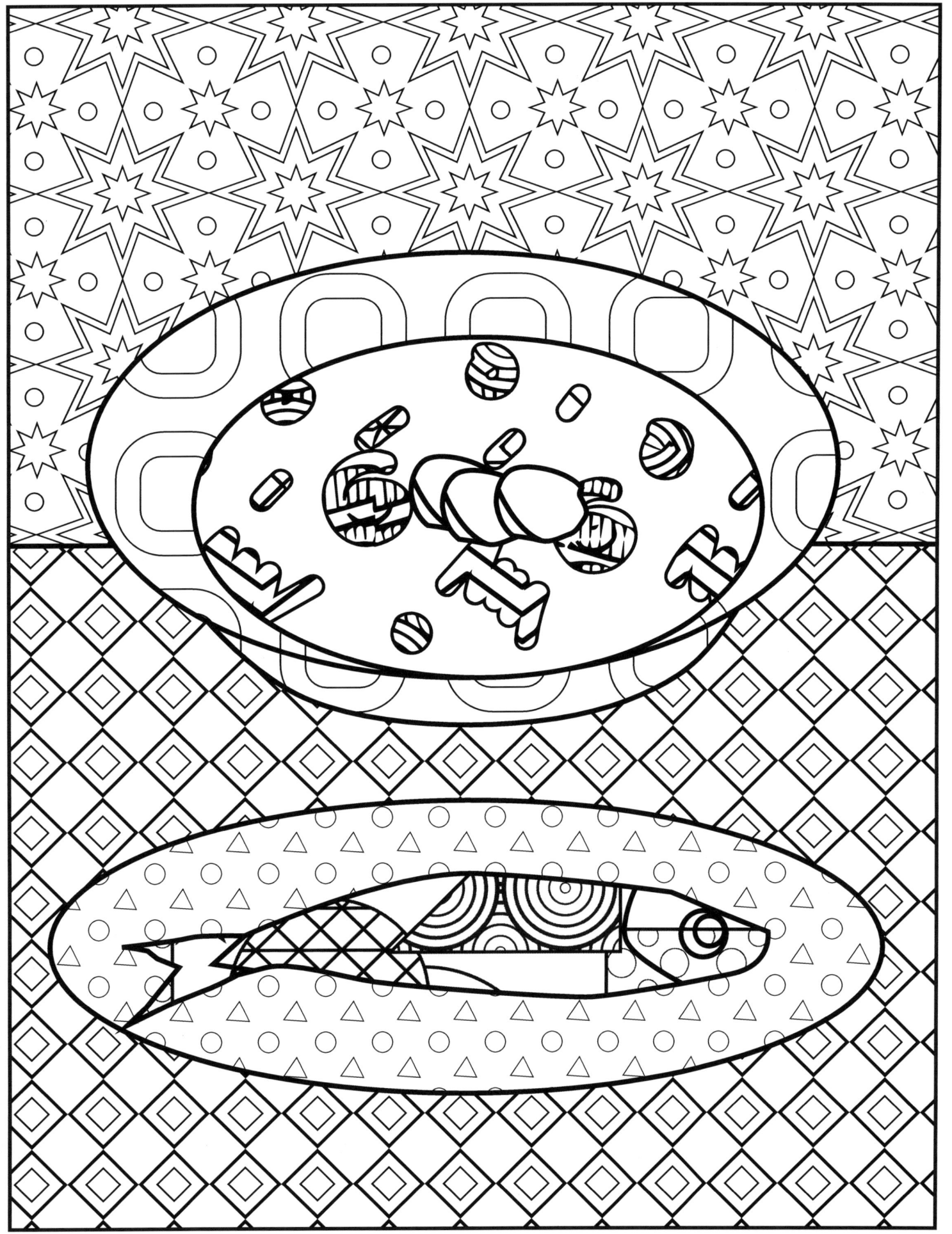

Manufactured by Amazon.ca
Bolton, ON

33839817R00035